FLIES

For a free color catalog describing Gareth Stevens' list of high-quality books and multimedia programs, call 1-800-542-2595 (USA) or 1-800-461-9120 (Canada). Gareth Stevens Publishing's Fax: (414) 225-0377. See our catalog, too, on the World Wide Web: http://gsinc.com

Library of Congress Cataloging-in-Publication Data

Green, Tamara, 1945-
    Flies / by Tamara Green ; illustrated by Tony Gibbons.
      p. cm. -- (The New creepy crawly collection)
    Includes bibliographical references and index.
    Summary: Examines the anatomy, behavior, dangers, relatives, and enemies of the common house fly.
    ISBN 0-8368-1914-4 (lib. bdg.)
    1. Flies--Juvenile literature. 2. Flies as carriers of disease--Juvenile literature.
  [1. Flies.] I. Gibbons, Tony, ill. II. Title. III. Series.
QL533.2.G74 1997
595.77--dc21
                                             97-7335

This North American edition first published in 1997 by
Gareth Stevens Publishing
1555 North RiverCenter Drive, Suite 201
Milwaukee, Wisconsin 53212 USA

This U.S. edition © 1997 by Gareth Stevens, Inc. Created with original © 1996 by Quartz Editorial Services, 112 Station Road, Edgware HA8 7AQ U.K.

Additional illustrations by Clare Heronneau.

Consultant: Matthew Robertson, Senior Keeper, Bristol Zoo, Bristol, England.

Printed in Mexico

1 2 3 4 5 6 7 8 9 01 00 99 98 97

THE NEW CREEPY CRAWLY COLLECTION

FLIES

by Tamara Green
Illustrated by Tony Gibbons

Gareth Stevens Publishing
MILWAUKEE

Contents

Getting to know flies

In all, there are as many as 150,000 types of flies, and they can be found all around the world. But the kind that most of us know best is probably the housefly, with the scientific name *Musca domestica*. You'll often hear it buzzing against a window pane on a summer day or spot one circling under an electric light at night.

Many types of flies can bite, even though they appear harmless. They can also spread disease when they land on food. That's why we need to do all we can to keep our homes free of them.

Lots of flies, as you will discover in this book, are amazing creatures. They are superb acrobats and can even walk upside-down on the ceiling! Read on to find out how they manage this extraordinary trick.

5

In close-up

This ordinary housefly has been enlarged many times. Take a look at its head. What enormous eyes it has! They are very different from yours. Humans have just one lens in each eye. But, amazingly, the eyes of a housefly each have about four thousand six-sided lenses. With their eyes, flies can see almost all around themselves, but not very far into the distance. They can also recognize different colors and ultra-violet light, which is a type of light that is invisible to humans.

The fly has antennae, or feelers, on its head. They are small and hang down. Other bristles, too, stick out of its head.

All the hairs are very sensitive to vibrations, which is why a fly can sense your approach. As you move toward the fly, a wave of air moves ahead of you. This causes the hairs on the fly's head to vibrate and warn the fly, giving it an extra fraction of a second to escape.

Now take a look at the fly's mouth area. At the front, a long feeding tube, or proboscis, sticks out. This is used for sucking up liquids, much as you do when you drink through a straw. The housefly cannot digest lumps of solid food, so it takes in fluids mostly. On its proboscis, however, the fly also has mini teeth that it uses to bite off tiny bits of food. These bits are then softened by liquids that the fly regurgitates (brings up again).

Most flies have a pair of fully developed wings, which they use to fly. A pair of small knobby structures, called halteres, takes the place of a second, hind set of wings. They help the fly keep its balance. Some flies do not have wings at all. The housefly's six legs are long and slim, ending in padded feet. These are especially useful for walking upside-down on ceilings, as you will discover when you turn the page.

Amazing

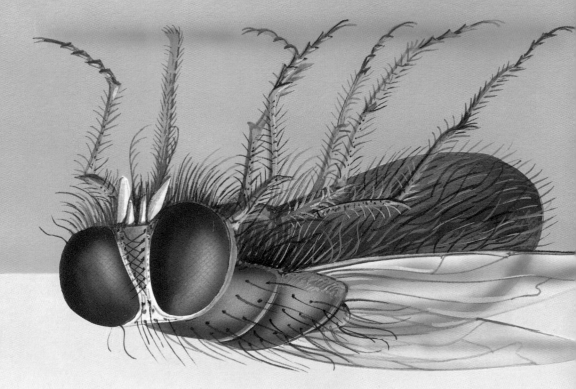

Unless you are a make-believe character like Batman, you find it impossible to climb up walls or walk across the ceiling of a room. To the ordinary fly, however, such acrobatics are a normal part of life. How do they do it? The secret lies in the sticky pads they have on the bottom of their feet. These give the flies a grip on all kinds of surfaces — horizontal or vertical. You may even spot them sometimes stretching their legs out and doing a half-spin to land upside-down on the ceiling. Flies are also amazingly quick while in flight. This makes

acrobats!

them very difficult to catch. Their wings are powered by a system of strong muscles in the thorax. Scientists estimate that the ordinary housefly may even beat its wings an astonishing two hundred times each second! Tiny flies, such as mosquitoes and midges (you can read about them later in this book), beat their wings at an even faster rate. A fly's halteres, the structures taking the place of its hind wings, help the insect maintain its balance and perform all these amazing tricks without wobbling or crashing.

Health hazard

Houseflies do not bite, but they can still be a danger because they spread germs. If you leave uncovered food on the kitchen table, and if there is a housefly nearby, chances are it will soon settle in to suck up some food. Houseflies also feed on sewage and excrement and may do so before flying in through a door or window. This means they sometimes carry disease.

Humans can quickly get sick with an upset stomach or diarrhea (a stomach illness that keeps victims running to the bathroom) if they eat or drink something on which flies have landed. Flies carry germs on their legs and also regurgitate (bring up) part of a previous nasty meal when they feed on substances inside a house. A single housefly can carry over a million bacteria on its legs, body, or proboscis.

Some of these germs cause food-poisoning or worse, so it is very important to control houseflies and keep them out of your home.

Be sure all food is covered; and, at a meal, don't let flies near your plate. Keep kitchen waste covered, too, because it will attract flies; and always empty the kitchen garbage and outside dumpsters regularly. Keep screens in good repair and open a door or window to shoo these unwanted guests outdoors if they somehow manage to get in.

Crane flies

Crane flies are interesting. In some areas of the world, they have the nickname "daddy longlegs." They received this name in honor of their delicate, thread-like limbs, which are unlike the legs of most other flies.

You will find crane flies during the summer mostly, in gardens or the countryside. And, if they get indoors, you may notice how attracted they are to electric light.

An adult crane fly does not eat or drink much and feeds just on nectar and water. But the growing larva (also known as a leather jacket) that will turn into a crane fly eats a great amount of plant stems and roots.

Their spindly legs trail so much that crane flies can easily be trapped in a spider's web as they fly past. They must beware of such traps.

Enemies that

Look out! These are two of our most deadly insect enemies — tsetse flies native to Africa. These flies spread many serious diseases, especially sleeping sickness.

Also known by the scientific name *Glossina*, tsetse flies love to feed on blood. Both sexes will bite human skin to get at the blood. As a result, the nasty parasites they carry can enter the human bloodstream, causing fever, swelling, coma, and sometimes even death.

As you can see in this picture, tsetse flies look somewhat different from the ordinary housefly. Tsetse flies are usually dark with a mixture of brown and cream spots, stripes, and other markings. They are also a little larger than houseflies and fold their wings, one over the other like the blades of a closed pair of scissors, when they are resting.

Houseflies, as you discovered earlier in this book, lay eggs; but tsetse flies do not. Instead, they are viviparous. This means that, after mating, females give birth to live larvae that burrow into the soil.

In the soil, before they become adults, the larvae have to pupate. In other words, each larva first changes into a pupa. During this stage, its body develops into maturity. This process takes about four weeks.

Each female tsetse fly produces about twelve larvae during its lifetime. Both males and females have a short lifespan — only about six months.

One of the tsetse flies you see enlarged here has a bulging red abdomen. That's because it has just sucked up its own weight in blood. How greedy it is!

bite

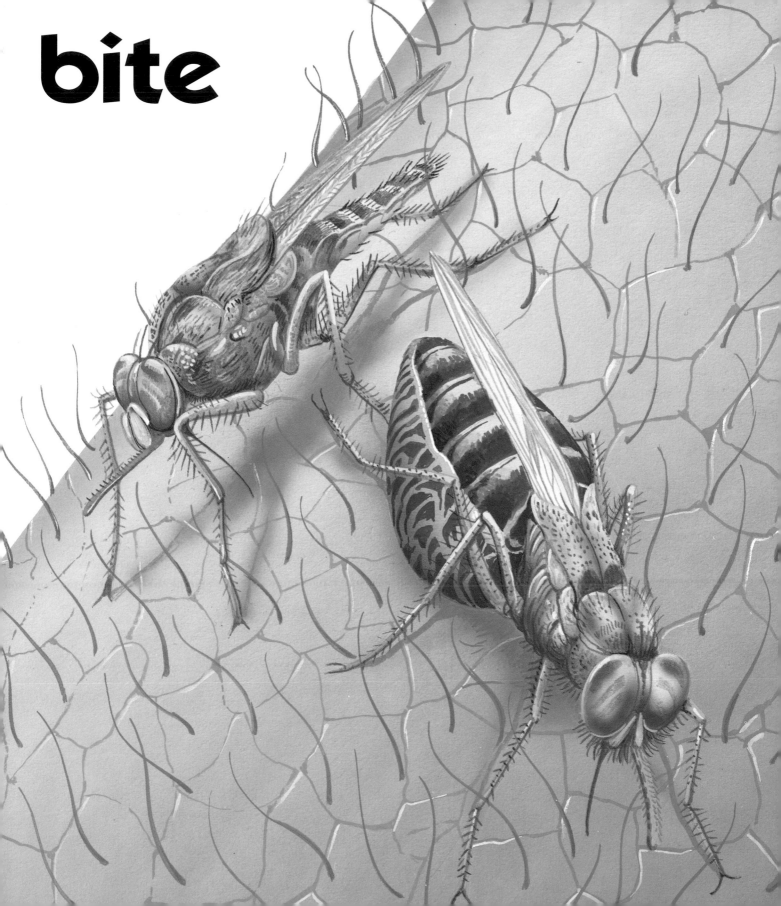

Birth of a

Summertime is when greenbottles usually mate. A male fly climbs on to a female's back, and they remain this way for a while.

A heap of garbage or the body of a dead creature is an ideal spot.

The eggs are tiny — only about the size of the period (.) at the end of this sentence — but there are over one hundred of them. They are soft, without a hard shell.

Then, when the male flies away, the female greenbottle finds somewhere suitable to lay its fertilized eggs.

In just a day or so, tiny larvae, known as maggots, emerge from the eggs. These maggots eventually turn into greenbottles.

greenbottle

First, the maggots will feed on the garbage or dead animal's body so they can grow. At this stage, they have no visible head, no legs, and no wings. After about a week, the maggots wriggle their way into soil. Their skin now begins to harden, and they shed it.

Inside each pupa, an adult greenbottle is still developing. It will take about a week for it to emerge from the pupa's shell. For a while, the young greenbottle is wet and cannot fly.

Once they have accomplished this, each maggot has become what is called a pupa.

But it soon dries, and the insect is ready to fly. Its new body is green and shiny.

Other types

When you are outside in warm weather, perhaps on a picnic, you may be annoyed by a swarm of tiny flies known as midges. In some regions of the world, these flies are called "no-seeums" because they are so small. You can see one greatly enlarged in the illustration on the *right*.

You may have noticed midges on a summer evening, hovering in groups over water. Some will attack mosquitoes to suck blood or they may damage crops such as wheat.

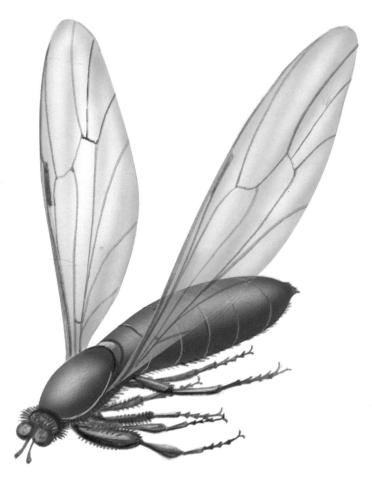

Other flies bite, too — the horsefly *left*, for example. It not only attacks horses but also humans, and its bite can be painful because its jaws are sharp. Horseflies can be a real nuisance; and, as with mosquitoes, it is the females that bite for blood.

# of flies

Hover flies, as their name suggests, tend to hover in the air. You will also see them gliding sideways, forward or backward, upward or downward. As you can see *below*, they look more like bees or wasps than true flies. They have boldly patterned bodies and make themselves useful by pollinating flowers. What big eyes they have! Listen for their song, too, as they buzz after settling.

Dance flies, like the ones *above*, get their name from the way the males dance as part of their courtship behavior. They also bring gifts to the females — usually another fly — which the females eat while mating. But the males are greedy and often snatch it away to give to another female before mating! Some will even kill their own species to give to a female, which is why they are also known as assassin flies.

19

Fighting flies

Houseflies are a nuisance and can carry germs. Some types of flies will even spread serious diseases. So humans need to keep flies under some sort of control.

Many methods have been tried in the attempt to get rid of flies. For example, some swampy areas have been drained of water. Also, a special chemical known as DDT has been used in the battle against mosquitoes — which spread the deadly disease of malaria. But mosquitoes soon became immune to the effects of DDT. Worse still, many fish, birds, and mammals were poisoned by this deadly chemical, so other insecticides were developed.

Scientists have even tried to eliminate some flies by sterilizing the males so they cannot fertilize the females. But flies are hardy. Besides, if all flies were destroyed, many bird species would starve.

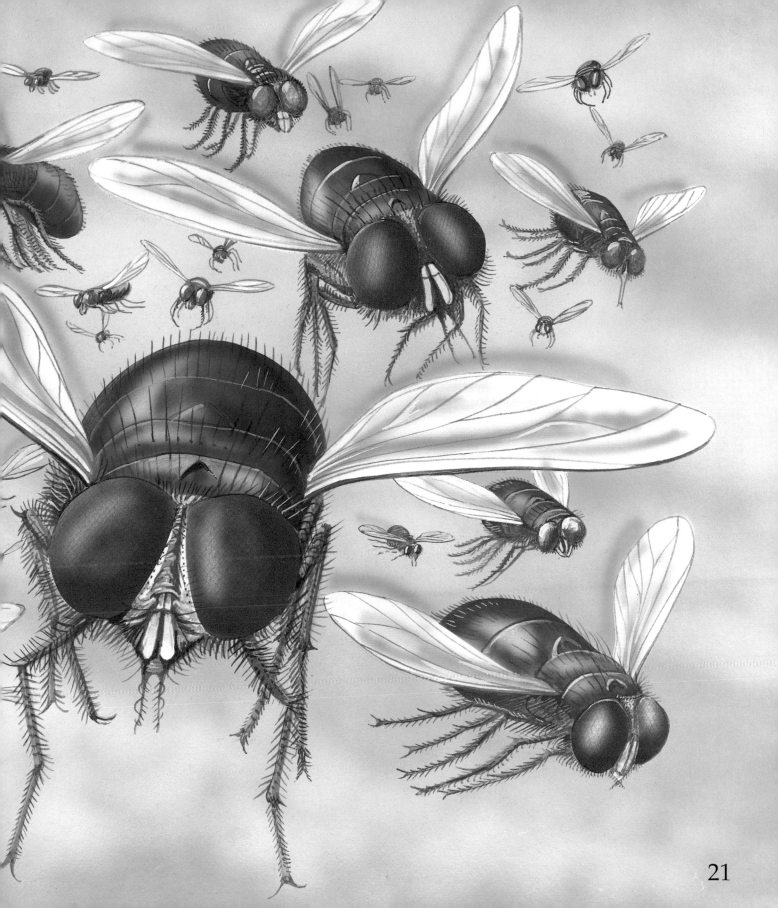

Did you know?

▲ *Are some flies predatory?*
It is true that some flies prey on other insects. The robber fly, for example, is predatory. It is a superb hunter that can catch other insects with its powerful legs while in flight. It then sucks the prey dry and drops the empty skin. Notice how the robber fly seems to have a beard and moustache. These bristles keep its face and eyes protected from the struggles of its victims.

How many eggs does a female housefly lay?
Houseflies may be responsible for a huge number of future generations. A female lays more than one hundred eggs at a time. In a single season, many millions of flies will come into existence as the final result of the original, single mating of just one male and one female fly.

What sort of diseases are spread by flies?
Among the illnesses spread by flies of various kinds are yellow fever, malaria, sleeping sickness, and food poisoning. Flies can also spread diseases that affect cattle, horses, camels, and several other animals.

Which are the biggest and smallest flies?
The biggest flies of all are about 3 inches (7.5 cm) long — about fifty times the size of the smallest, which is barely visible to the human eye.

Are flies insects?

All insects have a head with antennae, a thorax with three pairs of legs (six legs in all), and an abdomen. Usually, too, there are two pairs of wings. The housefly certainly has six legs, antennae, a thorax, and an abdomen. It has only one pair of wings to use for flying, so it belongs to a group called *Diptera*. Taking the place of a rear pair of wings are two stalked knobs, called halteres, that help with balance.

Where do houseflies go in winter?

Houseflies generally seem to disappear when winter comes to countries that have a cold season. They thrive most easily in the heat. But, even in freezing temperatures, a few survive by hibernating. In parts of the world where it is constantly hot, however, they are a nuisance all year round.

How fast can flies fly?

A scientist's reasonable guess is that some flies can travel at a speed of around 25 miles (40 km) per hour. This is about the average speed of a car in the city.

▼ Are any flies useful?

Some types of flies help pollinate flowers. Others produce larvae that feed on aphids which might otherwise destroy plants; and some will catch wasps or slugs.

What are a fly's main enemies?

Spiders, frogs, birds, and a few mammals that are insectivores prey on flies. But many flies can rely on camouflage to hide themselves, and will of course fly around very quickly to avoid being caught.

Glossary

abdomen — one of the three main body parts of an insect. The fly's abdomen is behind the thorax and contains the stomach.

aphids — tiny, soft-bodied insects, also known as plant lice, that suck juice from plants.

camouflage — a disguise that helps plants, animals, and humans blend in with their natural surroundings.

coma — a state of unconsciousness.

excrement — waste matter that living creatures produce.

insecticide — a poisonous chemical substance used to destroy insect pests, such as flies.

larva — a wingless, wormlike insect that is newly hatched.

malaria — a disease spread by a type of mosquito. People with malaria have chills, fever, and sweating.

nectar — a sweet liquid found in many flowers.

parasite — any animal that lives in or on another, and on which it feeds.

pupa — the stage of a fly's growth when it is still developing inside a cocoon.

thorax — the central section of an insect's body, which houses the heart.

Books and Videos

Amazing Insects. Laurence Mound (Knopf Books for Young Readers)

Flying Insects. WINGS series. Patricia Lantier-Sampon (Gareth Stevens)

Housefly. Heiderose Fischer-Nagel and Andreas Fischer-Nagel (Lerner Group)

Insects and Spiders. Penny Clarke (Watts)

Flies. (Journal Film and Video)

The Housefly. (Encyclopædia Britannica Educational Corporation video)

Index

24